Now We'll Make The Rafters Ring

Now We'll Make the Rafters Ring

Classic and Contemporary Rounds for Everyone

By
Edwin A. Finckel

Illustrated by
Dave Morice

a cappella books

Library of Congress Cataloging-in-Publication Data

Now we'll make the rafters ring: classic and contemporary rounds for
   everyone / [compiled and edited by] Edwin A. Finckel: illustrated
   by David Morice.
      p. of music.
      ISBN 1-55652-186-3 $11.95
      1. Glees, catches, rounds, etc.   I. Finckel, Edwin A.
   II. Morice, Dave, 1946-
   M1495.N93   1993   92-43866
                                                            CIP
                                                            M

a cappella books

an imprint of Chicago Review Press, Inc.

Editorial office:
POB 380
Pennington, NJ 08534

Business/sales office:
814 N. Franklin St.
Chicago, IL 60610

CONTENTS

Intermediate

Difficult

PREFACE

To me, rounds are one of the most delightful and educational musical forms to use as an introduction to choral singing. They give a wonderful start in the development of the ability to sing individual vocal lines. Each round is an exercise in both rhythm and pitch, especially when performed a cappella.

I've found it to be most helpful to have the group sing the melody in unison a few times followed by a trial run in two parts.

The numbers on the music indicate where each voice enters. The "holds" suggest a stopping place for the whole group after each group has completed the entire round, or each group can drop out while one group or voice sings to the end.

I've divided the book into three parts: easy (for ages five and up), intermediate (for ages eight and up), and difficult (for ages twelve and up). Within each section, though, the order is arbitrary, so feel free to skip around.

Rounds including a "foot" or "fres" should be used at the leader's discretion. The "foot" usually employs a second group of singers and can be used either as a start to the round or introduced during the round at any of the indicated starting places and continued to the end of the round.

Have fun!

EASY

Flip through this book and watch the notes dance along the left sides of the pages!

WAKE AND SING

MODERATELY FAST

WAKE AND SING,

2. WAKE AND SING,

3. COME AND JOIN OUR JOY - FUL MEA - SURE,

4. WAKE AND SING!

COME, FOLLOW

LADY BUG

Edwin A. Finckel

FAST

LA-DY-BUG, LA-DY-BUG, OH SO TI-NY

OH SO SWEET. LA-DY-BUG, LA-DY-BUG,

DO YOU WALK ON LEGS AND FEET? LA-DY-BUG,

LA-DY-BUG, I THINK YOU ARE REAL-LY NEAT!

JACK, BOY, HO, BOY

MODERATELY FAST

JACK, BOY, HO, BOY, NEWS!

2. NEWS! THE CAT IS IN THE WELL!

3. LET US RING NOW FOR HER KNELL,

4. DING, DONG, DING, DONG, BELL.

GREAT TOM IS CAST

MODERATELY FAST

GREAT TOM IS CAST, AND

CHRIST CHURCH BELLS RING ONE TWO THREE FOUR FIVE

SIX AND TOM COMES LAST.

LARGE CLOCKS

MODERATELY FAST

LARGE CLOCKS MARK TIME SLOW - LY,

TICK - TOCK, TICK - TOCK.

2.
SMALL CLOCKS MARK TIME FAS - TER,

TICK-TOCK, TICK-TOCK, TICK - TOCK, TICK - TOCK.

3.
AND THE LIT - TLE WATCH - ES MARK TIME,

TICK-Y TOCK-Y TICK-Y TOCK-Y TICK-Y TOCK-Y TICK.

DEAR FRIEND

MODERATELY SLOW

DEAR FRIEND, DEAR FRIEND, LET ME TELL YOU

HOW I FEEL. YOU HAVE GIV-EN ME SUCH PLEAS-URE

I LOVE YOU SO.

MY GOOSE

MODERATELY FAST

WHY SHOULD-N'T MY GOOSE SING AS WELL AS

THY GOOSE WHEN I PAID FOR MY GOOSE

TWICE AS MUCH AS THOU.

THE HEDONIST

HUMPTY DUMPTY

Edwin A. Finckel

RATHER FAST

HUMP-TY DUMP-TY SAT ON A WALL.

2.
HUMP-TY DUMP-TY HAD A GREAT FALL.

3.
ALL THE KING'S HOR-SES AND ALL THE KING'S MEN,

4.
COULD-N'T PUT HUMP-TY TO-GETH-ER A-GAIN.

THREE BLIND MICE

SHALOM HAVAYREEM

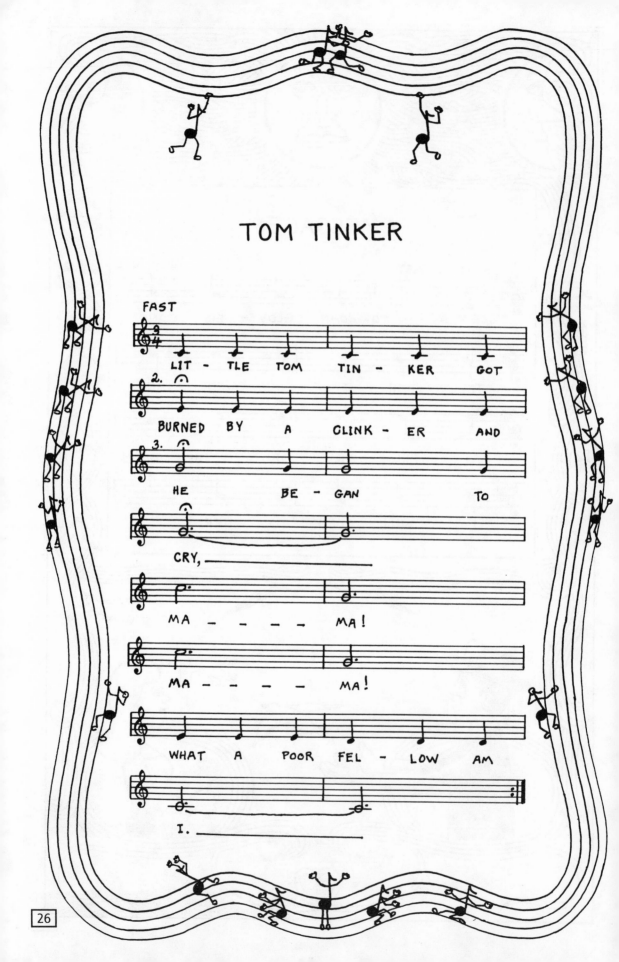

DO, RE, MI, FA

MODERATELY FAST

DO, RE, MI, FA,

I'M QUITE TIRED OF THIS SOL - FA - ING,

I FOR-GOT ALL YOU'VE BEEN SAY - ING.

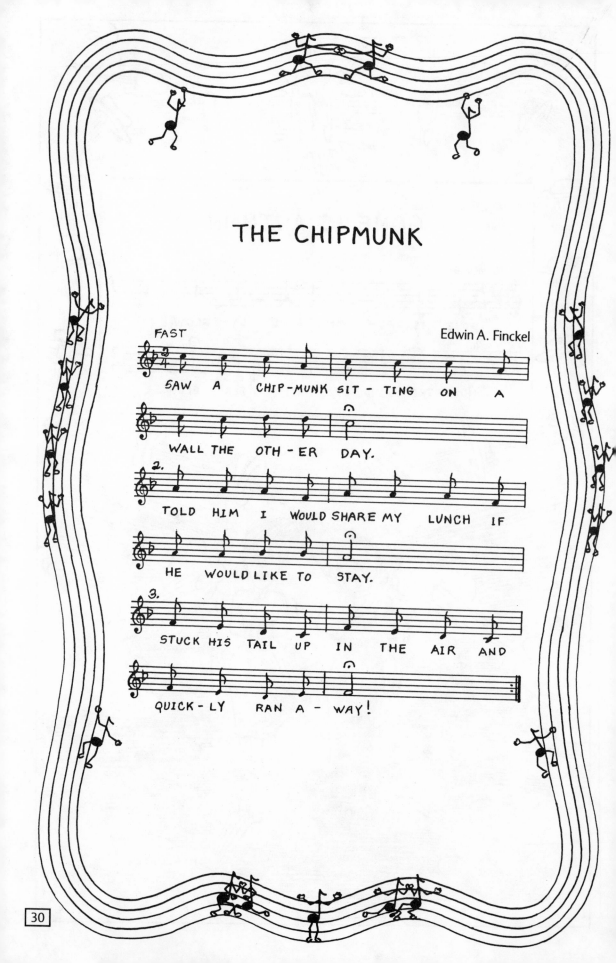

THE CHIPMUNK

Edwin A. Finckel

FAST

SAW A CHIP-MUNK SIT - TING ON A

WALL THE OTH - ER DAY.

2. TOLD HIM I WOULD SHARE MY LUNCH IF

HE WOULD LIKE TO STAY.

3. STUCK HIS TAIL UP IN THE AIR AND

QUICK - LY RAN A - WAY!

OH HOW LOVELY IS THE EVENING

MODERATELY FAST

OH,   HOW   LOVE –   LY

IS   THE   EVE –   NING,

IS   THE   EVE –   NING,

2.

WHEN   THE   BELLS   ARE

SWEET –   LY   RING –   ING,

SWEET –   LY   RING –   ING,

3.

DING,   DONG,

DING,   DONG,

DING,   DONG.

NOW THE DAY IS NEARLY DONE

RATHER SLOW

NOW THE DAY IS NEAR-LY DONE,

2. NIGHT IS SLOW-LY COM-ING ON,

3. SWEET-LY SLEEP TILL MORN-ING LIGHT:

4. GOOD - NIGHT! GOOD - NIGHT!

INTERMEDIATE

SWEETLY FLOW

MODERATELY SLOW

Hayes 1788

SWEET - LY FLOW THOU GEN - TLE STREAM ON WHOSE BANKS _____ FRESH _____ BEAU - TIES BEAM.

LITTLE PETE

RATHER FAST

Edwin A. Finckel

TWEET, TWEET, TWEET, HEAR THE TWEET, TWEET, TWEET, HEAR THE

TWEET OF THE BIRD IN THE TREE.   I WILL CALL HIM

2.

PETE, PETE, PETE, LIT-TLE PETE, PETE, PETE, LIT-TLE

PETE, LIT-TLE PETE, LIT-TLE PETE.   THIS IS VER-Y

3.

NEAT, NEAT, NEAT, VER-Y   NEAT, NEAT, NEAT, VER-Y

NEAT, VER-Y NEAT, VER-Y   NEAT. OH LIS-TEN TO THE

OH MUSIC, SWEET MUSIC

RATHER FAST

OH, MUS - IC, SWEET MUS - IC, THY

PRAIS - ES WE SING, 2. WE'LL

TELL OF THE PLEA - SURE AND

GLAD - NESS YOU BRING, 3.

MUS - IC, MUS - IC,

GLAD - NESS YOU BRING.

AH MY HEART

Clemens 1475
Set by Herman Reichenbach

MODERATELY SLOW

AH MY HEART WHAT AIL — ETH THEE TO

SET SO LIGHT MY LI — BER-TY? MAK — ING BONDS WHEN

I WAS FREE? MY HEART WHAT AIL — ETH THEE? WHAT

AIL — ETH THEE?

POOR MISS BROWN

RATHER FAST

Edwin A. Finckel

POOR MISS BROWN HAD A DREAD-FUL FROWN, WHEN SHE SMILED HER LIPS TURNED DOWN, BUT

2. THEN ONE DAY ON A TRIP TO TOWN, SOME-ONE TURNED HER UP-SIDE DOWN. SO

3. NOW SHE SMILES, DOESN'T HAVE A FROWN. SHE'S A HAP-PY POOR MISS BROWN.

THE ORCHESTRA

MODERATELY FAST

Edwin A. Finckel

UP AND DOWN BOW THE STRINGS. THEN YOU

TOOT TOOT TOOT ON THE FLUTE. PLAY A

2. BLEEP BLEEP BLEEP ON THE PRET-TY CLAR-IN-NET.

BLAP BLAP BLAP ON THE TRUM-PET SHIN-Y BRIGHT.

3. HONK HONK HONK THE TU-BA'S VER-Y FAT.

BOOM BOOM BOOM THE TYM-PA-NI IS GREAT!

HOW GREAT IS THE PLEASURE

MODERATELY FAST

HOW GREAT IS THE PLEAS - URE HOW
SWEET THE DE - LIGHT, WHEN
FRIEND - SHIP AND MU - SIC TO -
GETH - ER U - NITE. HOW
GREAT IS THE PLEAS - URE HOW
SWEET THE DE - LIGHT, WHEN
FRIENDS IN SONG TO -
GETH - ER U - NITE.
SWEET, SWEET, HOW

How Great Is the Pleasure, con't.

SWEET THE DE - LIGHT, WHEN

HAR-MO- NY, SWEET HAR- MO - NY, AND

FRIEND - SHIP U - NITE.

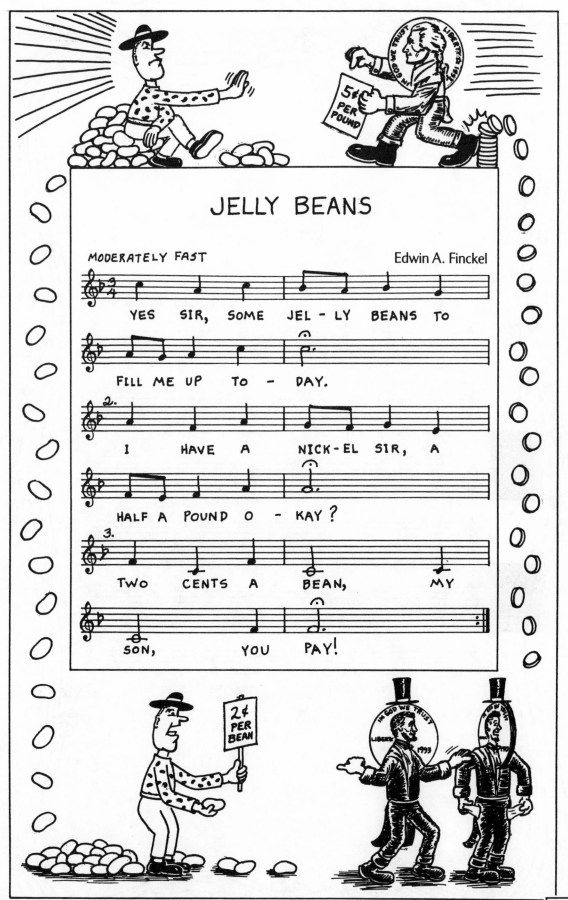

HEY HO

Byrd 1543

RATHER SLOW

HEY HO, TO THE GREEN-WOOD NOW LET US

GO, SING HEAVE AND HO; AND THERE SHALL WE

FIND BOTH BUCK AND DOE, SING HEAVE AND HO; THE HART AND

HIND AND THE LIT-TLE PRET-TY ROE, SING HEAVE AND HO.

KERPLOP

Edwin A. Finckel

RATHER FAST

I WILL CLIMB A TREE, JUST YOU WAIT AND SEE.

NOW I'M AT THE TOP, HERE I COME KER-PLOP!

MAZE TREE

KER-PLOP!

DONA NOBIS PACEM

RAIN

Edwin A. Finckel

FAST

RAIN, RAIN, RAIN, RAIN,

HOW I LOVE TO HEAR THE RAIN

2.

MAK — ING ALL THE FLOW — ERS GROW,

MAK — ING ALL THE RIV — ERS FLOW.

3.

IF YOU FIND YOU CAN — NOT STAY,

COME A — GAIN AN — OTH — ER DAY.

NIGHTINGALES

MODERATELY SLOW

Anon

ALL IS SI – LENT; NIGHT – IN –

GALES _____ SING SO SWEET – LY TEN – DER MEL – O – DIES,

DRAW TEARS FROM OUR EYES, SIGHS FROM THE HEART, SING SO SWEET – LY

TEN – DER MEL – O – DIES, DRAW TEARS FROM OUR EYES, SIGHS FROM THE HEART.

BE WELCOME

EASY SWINGING STYLE

Franz Schubert

BE WEL-COME GEN-TLE MONTH OF MAY WITH

WREN AND ROB-IN'S ROUN-DE-LAY; BE

WEL-COME GEN-TLE MONTH OF MAY WITH

WREN AND ROB-IN'S ROUN-DE-LAY; BE

WEL-COME GEN-TLE MONTH OF MAY WITH

WREN AND ROB-IN'S ROUN-DE-LAY.

WHAT CAN YOU BUY ?

MODERATELY FAST JAZZ BEAT

Edwin A. Finckel

YOU'VE GOT A PEN-NY,___ WHAT CAN YOU BUY?

ONE PRET-TY RAIN-BOW,___ HIGH IN THE SKY.___

2. YOU'VE GOT A NICK-EL, WHAT CAN YOU BUY?___

FIVE LIT-TLE MOON-BEAMS, RIGHT IN YOUR EYE.___

3. DON'T HAVE ONE CENT WHAT CAN YOU BUY?___

LOTS OF LOVE, JUST GIVE IT A TRY!___

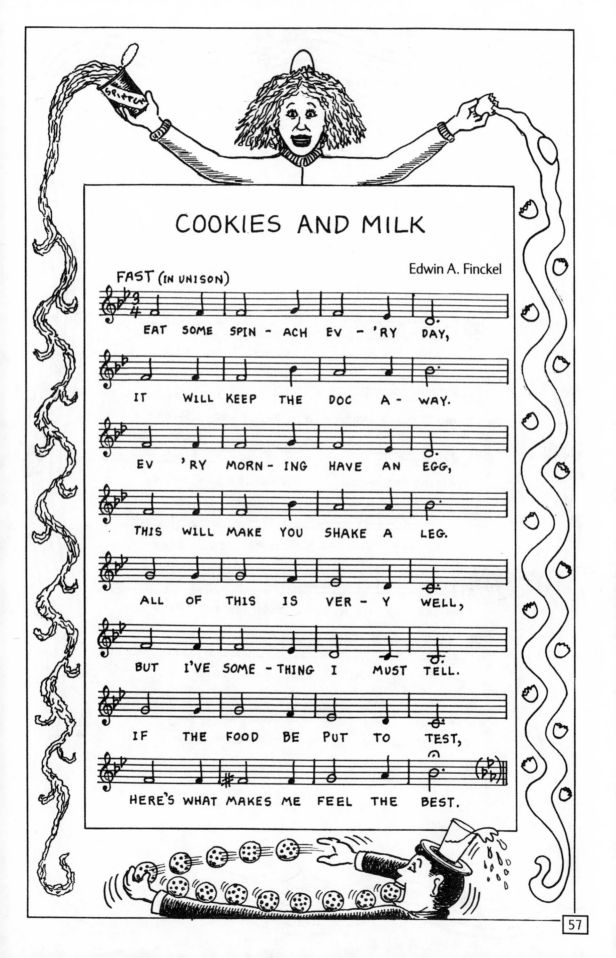

COOKIES AND MILK

Edwin A. Finckel

FAST (IN UNISON)

EAT SOME SPIN - ACH EV - 'RY DAY,

IT WILL KEEP THE DOC A - WAY.

EV 'RY MORN - ING HAVE AN EGG,

THIS WILL MAKE YOU SHAKE A LEG.

ALL OF THIS IS VER - Y WELL,

BUT I'VE SOME - THING I MUST TELL.

IF THE FOOD BE PUT TO TEST,

HERE'S WHAT MAKES ME FEEL THE BEST.

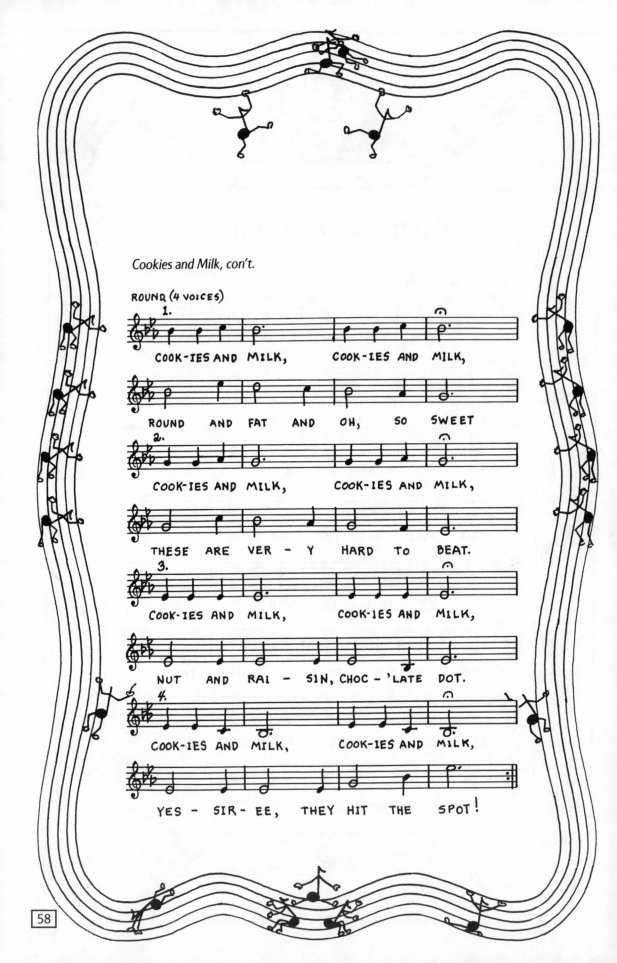

Cookies and Milk, con't.

ROUND (4 VOICES)

1.
COOK-IES AND MILK, COOK-IES AND MILK,

ROUND AND FAT AND OH, SO SWEET

2.
COOK-IES AND MILK, COOK-IES AND MILK,

THESE ARE VER-Y HARD TO BEAT.

3.
COOK-IES AND MILK, COOK-IES AND MILK,

NUT AND RAI-SIN, CHOC-'LATE DOT.

4.
COOK-IES AND MILK, COOK-IES AND MILK,

YES-SIR-EE, THEY HIT THE SPOT!

PIGGLY WIGGLY

MODERATELY FAST

Edwin A. Finckel

PIG - GLY WIG - GLY WHAT DOES IT MEAN?

PIG - GLY WIG - GLY I'VE NEV - ER SEEN.

IS IT A PIG - GY OR IS IT A WORM?

DON'T EV - ER TOUCH IT YOU MIGHT MAKE IT SQUIRM.

IF I SHOULD SEE ONE I'LL TELL YOU MORE.

GRAND - MOTH - ER SAYS IT'S A GROCE - RY STORE!

PSALM 66

MODERATELY FAST   Set by Herman Reichenbach

MAKE A JOY - FUL NOISE UN - TO GOD,

ALL YE LANDS. SING FORTH THE HON - OR

OF___ HIS_____ NAME; MAKE___

___ HIS PRAISE___ GLO - RI - OUS.

ALLELUIA

MODERATELY FAST

AL - LE - LU - IA, AL - LE -
LU - IA, A - - - - MEN,
A - - - MEN.

HYMNUS ANGELICUS

Gebhardi 1789
Set by Herman Reichenbach

FAST

GLO-RY TO GOD   IN THE   HIGH — EST!

AND ON — EARTH — PEACE; — AND —

GOOD WILL, GOOD WILL — TOWARD — MEN. A —

— — — MEN, A — — — MEN.

The Forgotten Rag Doll, con't.

ROUND. (FOUR VOICES)   (VOICE 1.)

LIT - TLE   RAG   DOLL   DON'T   YOU   CRY,   YOUR

2. FRIEND   HAS   LEFT   WITH   NO   GOOD - BYE.

3. AS   SHE   LEFT   I   HEARD   HER   SAY,   THAT

4. SHE'D   COME   BACK   FOR   YOU   ONE   DAY.

THE COOL OF AUTUMN

DIRGE

WHITE IS THE SNOW

NOT TOO FAST

WHITE IS THE SNOW, GREEN IS THE GRASS,

BLUE IS THE SKY, BLACK IS THE NIGHT.

WHITE, BLACK, BLUE, GREEN

ARE THE PRET-TI—EST COL-ORS THAT WERE EV-ER SEEN.

I WONDER WHO INVENTED THE ICE CREAM CONE

RATHER FAST

Edwin A. Finckel

I WON-DER WHO IN - VEN - TED THE ICE CREAM

2.

CONE. IT MUST HAVE BEEN A SNOW-MAN WHO

3.

MADE HIS OWN. I THINK THAT I WILL

CALL HIM ON THE TEL - E - PHONE.

FROSTY'S CONES

THE METRONOME

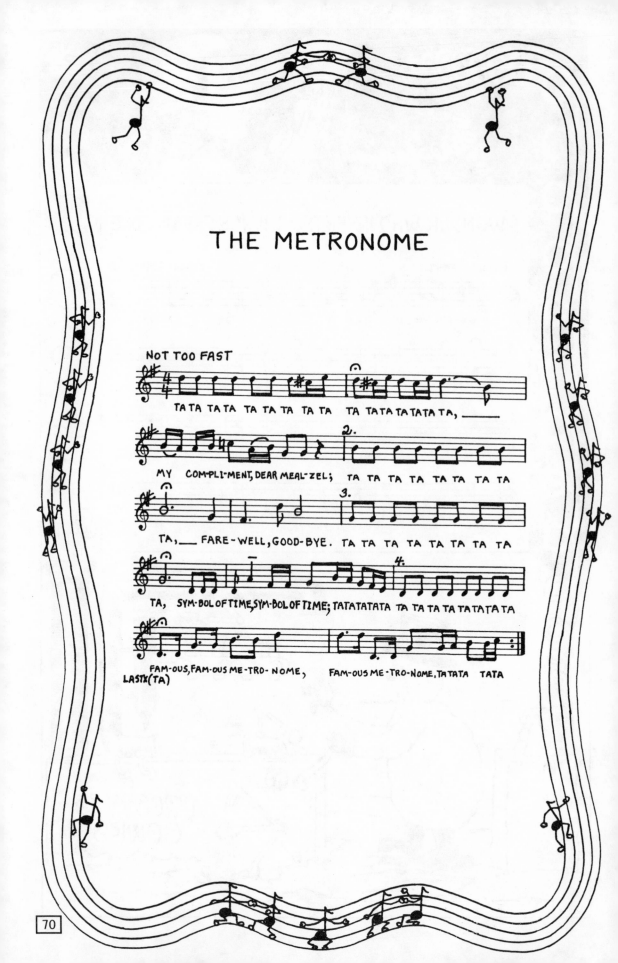

SOMEONE LOVES YOU

MODERATELY SLOW

Edwin A. Finckel

WHEN YOU'RE FEEL — ING

ALL A - LONE, YOU

MUST RE — MEM — BER

THIS, MY CHILD, THERE'S AL - WAYS

SOME - ONE ———— WHO LOVES YOU

VER - Y MUCH. AND SO————

DIFFICULT

WHO KNOWS ?

MODERATELY FAST   Edwin A. Finckel

WHO KNOWS THE NUM - BER OF THE BEATS I'M

COUNT - ING ? YOU MUST BE VER - Y STEAD - Y.

YOU'LL NEV - ER KNOW UN - TIL YOU SING IT.

TRY IF YOU CAN TO REAL - LY SWING IT.

I'LL HELP YOU COUNT IF YOU ARE READ - Y,

ONE, TWO AND THREE AND FOUR AND FIVE AND

(FOOT)

ONE, TWO, THREE, FOUR, FIVE.

SUMMER IS YCOMEN IN

RATHER FAST

SUM-MER IS Y-COM-EN IN,____

2.
LOUD-LY SING CUCK-OO!

3.
GROW-ETH SEED, AND BLOW-ETH MEAD, AND

4.
SPRING-ETH WOOD A-NEW.

SING CUCK-OO,

EWE NOW BLEAT-ETH AF-TER LAMB, LOW'TH

AF-TER CALF THE COW;

BUL-LOCK START-ETH, BUCK NOW VERT-ETH,

MER-RY SING CUCK-OO

Summer Is Ycomen In, con't.

CUCK - OO,   CUCK - OO,

WELL SING'ST THOU CUCK - OO   AND____

CEASE THOU NEV - ER   NOW.

(FRES)

SING   CUCK - OO   NOW____

SING   CUCK - OO.

The fres (or foot) can be used as a fifth voice or as an introduction and sung throughout the round.

TEACHER, TEACHER

MODERATELY FAST

Edwin A. Finckel

TEACH — ER, TEACH — ER, WILL YOU HELP ME TIE MY SHOE?

2. I HAVE TRIED IT FIF-TY TIMES, CAN YOU TELL ME WHAT TO DO?

3. JOHN-NY, LET ME SHOW YOU HOW, IT WILL NOT BE HARD FOR YOU,

4. O — VER, UN — DER, LEFT AND RIGHT, MAKE A LOOP AND PULL IT THRU.

5. NOW YOU TRY IT BY YOUR-SELF. YOU WILL FIND IT EAS-Y TOO.

6. THANK YOU TEACH-ER HERE WE GO, I CAN DO IT WHOOP-DE -DOO!

JINKIN THE JESTER

FAST

JINK-IN THE JEST - ER WAS WONT TO MAKE

GLEE WITH JAR - VIS THE JUG - GLER 'TIL

AN - GRY WAS HE. WHEN WIL - KIN THE

WISE MAN DID WISE-LY FORE - SEE THAT

JUG - GLER AND JEST - ER SHOULD GENT-LY A -

GREE. HEY DOWN, DOWN, DOWN, DOWN, DER-RY

DOWN, DOWN, DER-RY DOWN DOWN.

CATCH

RATHER FAST

Purcell

I GAVE HER CAKES AND I GAVE HER

ALE, AND I GAVE HER SACK AND

SHER — RY; _____ I KISSED HER

ONCE AND I KISSED HER TWICE, AND

WE ___ WERE WOND — 'ROUS MER — RY. _____

2.

_____ I GAVE HER BEADS AND

BRACE — LETS FINE, AND I GAVE HER

GOLD DOWN DER — RY; _____ I

THOUGHT SHE WAS A — FEARD TILL SHE STRUCK MY

Catch, con't.

BEARD   AND   WE   WERE   WOND – 'ROUS

3.

MER – RY; _____   MER-RY MY HEARTS,

MER – RY   MY COCKS, MER – RY   MY SPRITES,

MER-RY, MER – RY, MER-RY, MER-RY, MER-RY, MY

HEY   DOWN DER – RY; _____   I

KISSED HER   ONCE, AND I   KISSED   HER

TWICE,   AND   WE   WERE   WOND – 'ROUS

MER – RY. _____

BUY MY DAINTY FINE BEANS

MODERATELY SLOW

BUY MY DAIN-TY FINE BEANS, BUY MY BEANS. BUY MY

DAIN-TY FINE BEANS, BUY MY BEANS.

2.

CRAB, CRAB, BUY MY CRAB.

CRAB, CRAB, BUY MY CRAB.

3.

HOT, HOT MUT-TON PIES.

HOT, HOT MUT-TON PIES.

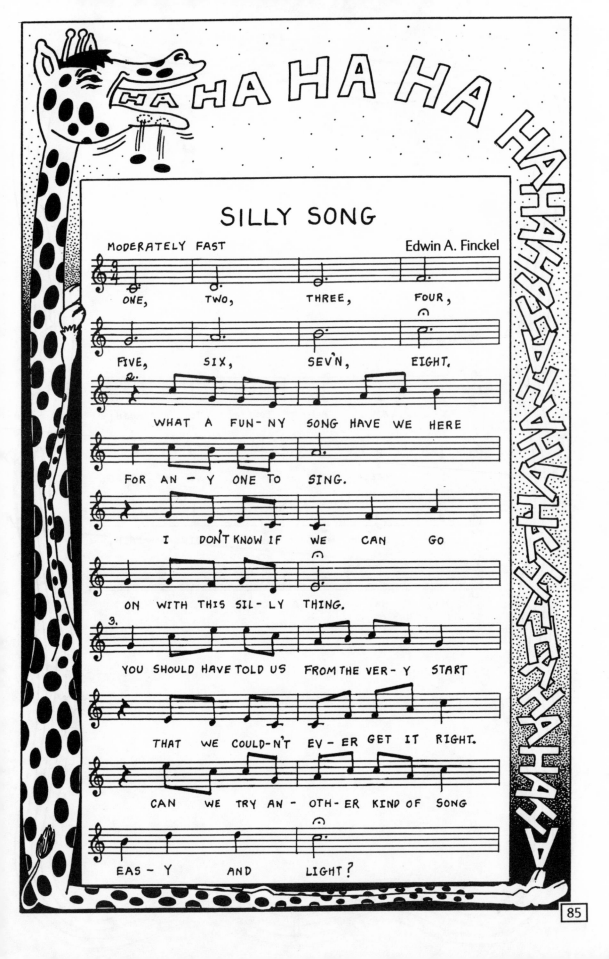

SILLY SONG

Edwin A. Finckel

MODERATELY FAST

ONE, TWO, THREE, FOUR,

FIVE, SIX, SEV'N, EIGHT.

WHAT A FUN-NY SONG HAVE WE HERE

FOR AN-Y ONE TO SING.

I DON'T KNOW IF WE CAN GO

ON WITH THIS SIL-LY THING.

YOU SHOULD HAVE TOLD US FROM THE VER-Y START

THAT WE COULD-N'T EV-ER GET IT RIGHT.

CAN WE TRY AN-OTH-ER KIND OF SONG

EAS-Y AND LIGHT?

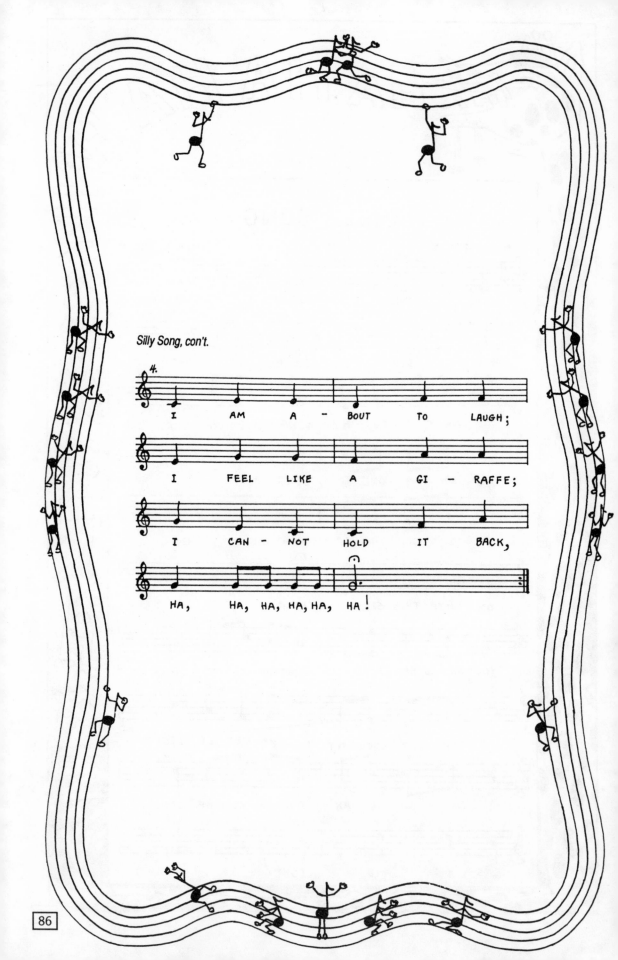

Silly Song, con't.

4.

I AM A - BOUT TO LAUGH;

I FEEL LIKE A GI - RAFFE;

I CAN - NOT HOLD IT BACK,

HA, HA, HA, HA, HA, HA!

86

AVE MARIA

MY SWING

With an easy swing

Edwin A. Finckel

UP AND DOWN UP AND DOWN ME AND MY

SWING, FLY - ING SO HIGH LIKE A

BIRD ON THE WING. I COULD SWING

ALL DAY LONG IF I HAD JUST ONE MORE LIT-TLE PUSH

BUT THERE'S NO-BOD-Y HERE WHAT SHALL I

DO? OH WHAT A SHAME I'M SLOW-ING DOWN

RIGHT TO A STOP! OH BUT HERE COMES

WIL-LIE WINK TO HELP ME NOW.

FIE NAY PRITHEE JOHN

RATHER FAST

FIE NAY PRITH-EE JOHN, DO NOT QUAR-REL MAN,

2. LET'S BE MER-RY AND DRINK A BOUT.

YOU'RE A ROGUE, YOU CHEAT-ED ME, I'LL PROVE BE-FORE THIS COM-PA-NY, I

CAREN'T A FAR-THING SIR, FOR ALL YOU ARE SO STOUT.

3. SIR YOU LIE, I SCORN YOUR WORD, OR AN-Y MAN WHO WEARS A SWORD, FOR

ALL YOUR HUFF WHO CARES A FIG AND WHO CARES FOR YOU!

UBI SUNT GAUDIA

MODERATELY FAST

U - BI SUNT GAU - DI - A 'TIS ON - LY WHERE

AN - GELS SING NO - VA CAN - TIC - A AND

BELLS _____ RING IN RE - GIS

CU - RI - A. OH WERE WE THERE!

NOT A NIGHTINGALE

MODERATELY FAST · Brahms

1. HIGH ON A PINE TREE A LIT - TLE BIRD
2. NO SIR, THAT IS NOT A NIGHT - IN - GALE;

2.
RAIS - ES A HUL - LA - BA - LOO.
NO SIR YOU ARE OUT OF LUCK.

3.
WHICH BIRD IN - VENTS SUCH GREAT MEL - O - DIES?
NIGHT - IN - GALES DON'T SING ON AN - Y TREE

4.
THIS ON - LY NIGHT - IN - GALES DO.
BUT ON A HAZ - EL - NUT SHRUB.

DEATH IS A LONG, LONG SLEEP

RATHER SLOW

DEATH IS A LONG _____

_____ LONG SLEEP.

SLEEP IS A SHORT SHORT

DEATH WHICH SOF-TENS, BUT DEATH

STOPS LIFE'S GRIEF, DEATH IS A

LONG LONG SLEEP.

AVE MARIA

W. A. Mozart 1756

TO NIGHT

Moderately slow

Mozart (Shelley)

SWIFT — LY

2. WALK O - VER THE WEST - ERN

3. WAVE, SPIR —

4. IT OF NIGHT! _____

5. _____ OUT OF THE MIST - Y, EAST - ERN

6. CAVE.

HARVEST ROUND

Popcorn, con't.

GIM-ME, GIM-ME, GIM-ME, GIM-ME

ONE MORE BITE AND THEN I'M GON-NA

BLOW UP, BLOW UP WITH A

(NOTE) ALL VOICES END ABRUPTLY AT THE FERMATA.

DO NOT HOLD THE NOTE.

THE HIKE

MODERATELY FAST

WHEN WILL THIS HIKE BE O - VER? I AM SO TIR'D OF

MARCH-ING, OF MARCH-ING, I AM SO DEAD-LY TIR'D. I'VE

LOST MY BEST COM - PAN-ION, MY PIPE, MY PAL, MY

FRIEND ON THE HIKE, FRIEND ON THE HIKE, MY

PRET-TY LIT-TLE MEER-SCHAUM PIPE. HUR-

RAY, HUR-RAY, I FOUND IT, I FOUND YOUR PAL, I

FOUND THE PIPE, FOUND THE PIPE, THUS

ON FOR-EV- ER GOES THE HIKE.

BONA NOX

MODERATELY FAST

W. A. Mozart

BO — NA NOX,

CHIME THE VIL - LAGE CLOCKS; BUO - NA

2. NOT - TE, MY DEAR LOT - TE; BONNE

NUIT, PHOOEY, PHOOEY; GOOD NIGHT, GOOD

3. NIGHT, THE STARS SHINE BRIGHT; GU-TE NACHT, GU-TE

NACHT, TURN OUT THE LIGHT; GOOD NIGHT!

4. SLEEP THOU WELL UN —

TIL I RING THE BELL.

YES, YES, NO, NO

I WILL NOT COUNT

Index by Title

Index by First Line